TWELVE reporters wait for the race to start.

twelve
12

1

ELEVEN autographs

decorate the program.

3

TEN spoilers glitter and gleam.

ten
10

5

NINE safety helmets
are strapped on tight.

nine
9

EIGHT binoculars follow the race.

eight
8

SEVEN pit workers surround a car.

9

SIX empty gas cans sit in a row.

FIVE racecars lead the pack.

five
5
••••

13

four
4
• • • •

FOUR wheels squeal around the turn.

15

THREE grandstands hold the fans.

three
3
...

17

TWO drivers race for the finish line.

ONE black-and-white checkered flag waves wildly.

THE WINNER!

Fun Facts

 The spoiler is on the back of the car. The spoiler pushes air down and helps the car's tires stay on the racetrack.

 Drivers wear helmets and special clothing that doesn't catch fire easily. Lap and shoulder belts also help keep drivers safe.

 The pit crew works quickly. It only takes seconds for the crew to fill the car with gas, change the tires, and get the car and driver ready to go back on the racetrack again.

 Race cars hold fuel in special tanks. The tanks contain foam or spongy materials to keep the fuel from spraying around if the cars crash.

 In 1977, Janet Guthrie became the first woman to race in the Indianapolis 500.

 Auto racing is one of the most popular sports in the world. People have been racing cars since cars were first built!

Find the Numbers

Now you have finished reading the story, but a surprise still awaits you.

Hidden in each picture is one of the numbers from 1 to 12. Can you find them all?

Key

12—on the purple car

11—on the metal band of the pencil

10—on the steering wheel of the second car from the left

9—on the yellow helmet

8—on the shirt on the man who is top left

7—on the leg of the woman on page 8

6—near the back of the car

5—back wheel of leading car

4—left front tire

3—front left corner of right grandstand section

2—back left tire on orange car

1—bottom right corner of flag person's stand

Go on an Observation Walk

Counting is fun! Step outside your door, and practice counting by going on an observation walk in your neighborhood—or even in your own yard. Ask an adult to go with you. On an observation walk, you notice the things all around you. Count the number of trees in your yard or on your block. Count the number of dogs you see. Count the number of windows on one side of your home. You can count everything!

Glossary

autograph—a person's handwritten name

binoculars—a device that makes far-away things look closer

grandstand—the place where those watching a race sit

spoiler—a part of the back of a car designed to use air to push down the car. The spoiler helps the tires grip the racetrack.

Index

On the Web

Fact Hound

Fact Hound offers a safe, fun way to find Web sites related to this book. All of the sites on Fact Hound have been researched by our staff.
http://www.facthound.com

1. Visit the Fact Hound home page.
2. Enter a search word related to this book, or type in this special code:1404805761.
3. Click on the FETCH IT button.

Your trusty Fact Hound will fetch the best sites for you!

Thanks to our advisers for their expertise, research, and advice:

Stuart Farm, M.A.
Mathematics Lecturer,
University of North Dakota
Grand Forks, North Dakota

Susan Kesselring, M.A.
Literacy Educator
Rosemount-Apple Valley-Eagan
(Minnesota) School District

The editor would like to thank Nichole Fredrickson Nelson of Elko Speedway for her expert advice in preparing this book.

Managing Editor: Bob Temple
Creative Director: Terri Foley
Editor: Brenda Haugen
Editorial Adviser: Andrea Cascardi
Copy Editor: Sue Gregson
Designer: Nathan Gassman
Page production: Picture Window Books
The illustrations in this book were rendered digitally.

Picture Window Books
5115 Excelsior Boulevard
Suite 232
Minneapolis, MN 55416
1-877-845-8392
www.picturewindowbooks.com

Printed in the United States of America.

Library of Congress Cataloging-in-Publication Data
Dahl, Michael.
One checkered flag : a counting book about racing / written by Michael Dahl ; illustrated by Derrick Alderman and Denise Shea.
p. cm. — (Know your numbers)
Summary: A counting book featuring things found at a car race, from one black-and-white checkered flag to twelve reporters. Readers are invited to find hidden numbers on an illustrated activity page. Includes bibliographical references and index.
ISBN 1-4048-0576-1 (reinforced lib. bdg.)
1. Automobile racing—Juvenile literature.
2. Counting—Juvenile literature.
[1. Automobile racing. 2. Counting. 3. Picture Puzzles.]
I. Alderman, Derrick, and Shea, Denise, ill. II. Title.
GV1029.13.D34 2004
796.72—dc22
                                          2003020969